# Contents

**Introduction** 1

**Management of health and safety** 3
Responsibility of the club 4
Training and competence 5
Reporting accidents and incidents 7

**Working environment** 9
The course 10
The golf professional's premises 12
Manual handling 13
Personal protective equipment (PPE) 14
Electrical safety 15

**Machinery** 19
Tractors 21
Power take-off (PTO) 23
Mowers 24
Turf scarifiers, slitters and spiking equipment 26
Groomers 26
Brush cutters, brush saws and grass trimmers 27
Fertiliser spreaders 28
Sand graders 29
Other machinery 30
Sprinkler systems 31
Personal transport 32

**Occupational health** 35
Hazardous substances 35
Use of pesticides 37
Noise and vibration 38

APPENDIX 1 **Know the law** 40
APPENDIX 2 **Guidance on course design** 48
APPENDIX 3 **References** 53
APPENDIX 4 **Further reading** 55
APPENDIX 5 **Other sources of information** 58

# HEALTH AND SAFETY in GOLF COURSE MANAGEMENT AND MAINTENANCE

HSE BOOKS

© Crown copyright 1994
Applications for reproduction should be made to HMSO
First published 1994

ISBN 0 7176 0689 9

The Health and Safety Executive would like to thank Wisley Golf Course for the assistance they provided with the photographs.

# INTRODUCTION

1   Most accidents on golf courses are associated with the use of agricultural machinery and pesticides. This guidance provides general information and advice for owners, managers and employees of golf courses about these areas.

2   The guidance describes the main risks found at golf courses and what should be done to safeguard the health and safety of employees and visitors. It will also be useful to golf club committees who have responsibilities, on behalf of the club, to employ staff and to maintain the course and buildings.

3   The guidance given in this note is not mandatory, but it does contain information on the health and safety responsibilities of those involved in the business. Employers may choose to take alternative effective steps if they wish.

4   The Health and Safety At Work etc Act 1974 and associated regulations will apply to golf course management and maintenance where there is a work activity and information on this is given in Appendix 1. For ease of reference, the law is set out in the order that it appears in the text.

5   Where British Standards are mentioned in the text, harmonised European Standards would also be appropriate.

# MANAGEMENT OF HEALTH AND SAFETY

6   Health and safety within any workplace needs to be managed and controlled to ensure that good standards are maintained and, where necessary, improved. The effective management of health and safety is key in preventing accidents and ill health at work.

7   Competent management systems include:

- setting a clear health and safety policy which covers the selection of people, equipment and materials, the way the work is to be done and what is required to do it safely;

- assessing the risk of certain hazards and practices found in the workplace;

- ensuring that adequate preventative measures are in place to control certain hazardous conditions and procedures;

- training staff in safe working practices;

- monitoring and reviewing those working practices; and

- effective communication with all those involved in managing and maintaining the golf course.

## RESPONSIBILITY OF THE CLUB

8   Golf clubs are normally managed by a committee or council supported by a number of sub-committees. As part of the management of health and safety, the committee would be responsible for ensuring that:

- employees and members are familiar with the club's safety policy and the arrangements to implement it;

- all employees are competent and trained and aware of the hazards in carrying out their duties;

- safety equipment and devices are properly used and maintained;

- machinery and equipment is properly maintained and safe to use;

- working practices are regularly reviewed to improve health and safety.

## TRAINING AND COMPETENCE

9   Training is one way of achieving health and safety competence and helps to convert information into safe working practices. Accident statistics show that many accidents occur when employees use machinery, equipment or substances without proper training and instruction.

10  All employees, including senior management, will need some training and information about health and safety. New employees (including volunteers and casual staff) should receive induction training on health and safety, including on how to operate machinery safely, using pesticides, emergency procedures, fire and evacuation. Also, a risk assessment may identify groups of workers especially at risk, such as young people and those employed on a casual basis for short periods each week, eg golf caddies.

11   The competence of staff should be monitored, especially as lack of job knowledge and skills can adversely affect health and safety. Any necessary update or refresher training should be provided. Special attention may need to be given to employees who deputise for others. Their skills are likely to be underdeveloped and they may need more help in understanding how to work in a safe and healthy way.

12   Further information and advice on training can be obtained from:

   ○ the Greenkeepers Training Committee;

   ○ local Training and Enterprise Councils who will be able to provide advice on National Vocational Qualifications. In Scotland, Local Enterprise Companies and Scottish Vocational Qualifications;

   ○ Agricultural Training Board - Landbase;

   ○ National Proficiency Tests Council;

   ○ colleges of further education.

13   There is also a HSE leaflet *Train to survive* [1] which provides general advice on training.

## REPORTING ACCIDENTS AND INCIDENTS

14  Certain injuries which occur at the workplace or as a result of work activities are reportable under the Reporting of Injuries, Diseases and Dangerous Occurrences Regulations 1985 (RIDDOR) (see Appendix 1). Deciding whether a particular incident or accident should be reported is often confusing. Below is a table showing typical accidents which occur at work and giving details of whether or not they are reportable under RIDDOR.

| Person involved | Accident details | Type of injury | Reportable under RIDDOR |
| --- | --- | --- | --- |
| Employee | Fell off step ladder while reaching for a box in the club's storeroom. Broke arm. | Major injury | Phone enforcing authority. Send form F2508 within 7 days. |
| Employee | Hurt back while lifting a piece of machinery. Off work for 5 days. | Over-3-day injury | Send F2508 to enforcing authority within 7 days. |
| Employee | Hurt back while digging garden at home. Off work for 5 days. | | Not reportable: accident not at work. |
| Visitor | Slipped on a wet surface in the clubhouse. Broke leg. | Major injury | Phone enforcing authority. Send F2508 within 7 days. |
| Visitor | Tripped over a poorly maintained floor covering. Off work for 4 days. | | Not reportable: over-3-day injuries only applicable to employees. |
| Employee or visitor | Any illness from absorption of any substance (including pesticide) needing medical treatment. | Major injury | Phone enforcing authority. Send F2508 within 7 days. |

15  In general, the nature of the injury determines whether it is major or over-3-day.

MANAGEMENT OF HEALTH AND SAFETY

# Working Environment

16 When creating a safe working environment, the following areas will need particular attention:

- the course, workshops and storage facilities;
- the golf professional's shop, including the workshop;
- working practices, such as manual handling and using electricity, and the need for personal protective equipment.

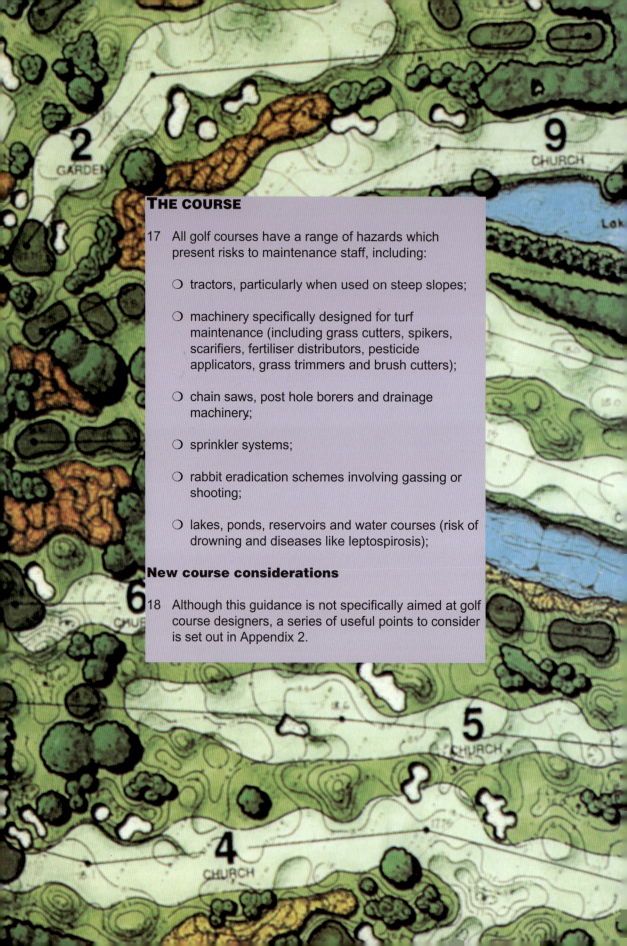

## THE COURSE

17  All golf courses have a range of hazards which present risks to maintenance staff, including:

- tractors, particularly when used on steep slopes;

- machinery specifically designed for turf maintenance (including grass cutters, spikers, scarifiers, fertiliser distributors, pesticide applicators, grass trimmers and brush cutters);

- chain saws, post hole borers and drainage machinery;

- sprinkler systems;

- rabbit eradication schemes involving gassing or shooting;

- lakes, ponds, reservoirs and water courses (risk of drowning and diseases like leptospirosis);

### New course considerations

18  Although this guidance is not specifically aimed at golf course designers, a series of useful points to consider is set out in Appendix 2.

# THE GOLF PROFESSIONAL'S PREMISES

19  The professional's shop is covered by the same legislation as other retail premises and the club has legal responsibilities relating to the provision, by them, of the professional's premises. The

workshop is also covered by health and safety legislation. For example, care needs to be taken if solvents (eg petrol) are used for cleaning in the shop or workshop. These may be flammable toxic or both, and their storage and use should be closely controlled. A licence from the fire authorities may be required for flammables such as petrol.

20  If professionals employ staff they will have the same legal responsibilities as any other employer in relation to their employees and to others who may be affected by their work activities.

## Manual handling

21 More than one quarter of all accidents reported to the HSE and local authorities each year arise from manual handling. Although the increased use of tractor driven and self-propelled machinery on golf courses has helped to reduce the need for manual handling, many courses will still use pedestrian controlled mowers which are often heavy and awkward to lift. Sprains and strains of backs and limbs are often sustained from manual handling and lifting. The injury may also be a result of cumulative damage often sustained over a considerable period, which can result in physical impairment or even permanent disability. Sprains and strains occur when bodily force is applied incorrectly. Poor posture is often a contributory factor.

22 When making an assessment of the manual handling operations at the course (see Appendix 1), there are four elements to be considered: the task, the load, the working environment and individual capability. It should be possible to complete the majority of assessments by you or your staff. For simple tasks, there is no reason for the assessment to be written down.

## Personal protective equipment (PPE)

23  Certain types of PPE will need to be supplied for golf course staff, particularly those working with dangerous machinery and hazardous substances (see Appendix 1).

24  PPE for use at golf courses might include:

- eye protection to guard against the hazard of splashes from pesticides, sprays and dust;

- ear protection to guard against excessive noise levels when using certain types of machinery, eg rotary mowers, chain saws;

- safety footwear to guard against the hazard of objects falling or crushing the foot and to protect against adverse weather, and machinery such as trimmers and hover mowers;

- gloves and, where necessary, arm protection to guard against cuts and abrasions, extremes of temperature, skin irritation and dermatitis and contact with pesticides and hazardous liquids;

- protective clothing for the body to guard against contact with pesticides and other hazardous substances, cold, heat and bad weather. Protective clothing and equipment should be worn when using machinery such as chain saws.

## ELECTRICAL SAFETY

25  Electricity can cause shocks, burns and start fires and can be fatal. The use of electrical equipment at golf courses is subject to the Electricity at Work Regulations 1989. One of the main requirements of the Regulations is that employers and self-employed persons maintain, so far as is reasonably practicable, electrical systems and electrical equipment within their control so as to prevent danger.

26  Electrical equipment within work premises should be installed and maintained by a competent person. If using an outside contractor, one way of demonstrating the contractor's competence would be to select an organisation who is a certificate holder of the National Inspection Council for Electrical Installation Contracting (NICEIC).

### Fixed electrical installations

27  All fixed electrical installations should be designed, installed, operated and maintained to prevent electrical danger. The Institution of Electrical Engineers (IEE) produces guidance on the construction of fixed installations in buildings and elsewhere. This is now in its sixteenth edition and is called the *Regulations for electrical installations*[2]. This is recognised as a British Standard (BS 7671:1992). It should be remembered that despite the title, these are *not* a legal requirement. The IEE also produces guidance on the inspection and testing of fixed installations.

**WORKING ENVIRONMENT**

## Portable equipment

28  Portable equipment, particularly items which are subject to strenuous use and hazardous conditions (ie water, grease), will need maintaining to ensure that it is safe for use. All equipment should be checked visually on a regular basis, to ensure that cables are in good condition, plugs are sound and correctly attached and the equipment is in general good repair. These checks should be part of an inspection programme but can also be undertaken by the user before and during use. Additionally, staff who have received training may be able to check the plug to see that a fuse is in use, and that cable terminations are secure and correct including the earth connection. However, no-one should carry out electrical work unless they have sufficient knowledge to prevent danger to themselves or others. It is not necessary to employ an electrician to carry out the visual checks. Testing by a competent person may be required under certain circumstances.

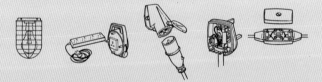

29  Hand-held electrical equipment used outdoors, or where there is a lot of earthed metalwork, should where possible be supplied at reduced voltage, ie 110 volt centre tapped earth (CTE) system from a safety isolating transformer. If this is not possible the equipment should be connected through a residual current device (RCD) which will cut off the power quickly if there is an earth fault. Such a fault could result in someone receiving an electric shock. The RCD should be checked monthly by pressing the test button.

30  Battery charging should be carried out in a well ventilated area away from sparks and other sources of ignition.

## Overhead lines

31  Electricity can flash over from overhead power lines to nearby objects, and the results can be lethal. There is particular danger to anyone working with a ladder, pole pruner or irrigation pipe close to an overhead line or on a tractor with loading bucket or any other equipment working near the line. *Avoidance of danger from overhead electrical lines* [3] provides further information. If sand, turf or other material is delivered to the golf course, it is essential that any load is tipped at least 10 metres from any line to avoid the risk of possible contact. Care also needs to be taken if digging holes in case of buried live cables. It is always advisable to contact the regional electricity company before starting any work close to overhead lines or buried cables.

# MACHINERY

32  Machinery can be dangerous. Important aspects in ensuring that machinery is used safely and without risk of fatal or serious accidents include: training, competence, maintenance, use of correct equipment and safe systems of work. Training provides staff with information on safe working practices and machines should only be used by someone who has been trained and is competent in their use. Competence can be developed by training and experience. To prevent unauthorised access, all machinery should be locked securely away when not in use and only employees of the club should have access to the workshop and garage areas.

33 Maintenance of machinery is essential. Safety devices, brakes, controls etc need regular maintenance. Guarding requirements have been developed to help prevent accidents which can happen when people get too close to dangerous parts of machines. In general, most guarding requirements are designed to prevent the operator and others from coming in contact with power driven components of machinery whilst in use. Machines are designed and fitted with guards to make them safe and it is essential that guards are not removed from machinery until all components come to rest. Machines should only be used if all guards are in place. *BS 5304:1988 Safety of machinery* [4] provides guidance on how to guard machinery effectively.

34 Machinery in use on golf courses can suffer build up of grass/debris around engine/transmission areas. This debris can absorb fuel, oil etc and eventually become a serious fire hazard. Cleaning at regular intervals will help to avoid this.

35 Most machines used on golf courses are driven by petrol or diesel-fuelled engines. Ensuring that all staff are adequately instructed in the safe use, transport and storage of petrol and diesel will help to prevent injuries and fire.

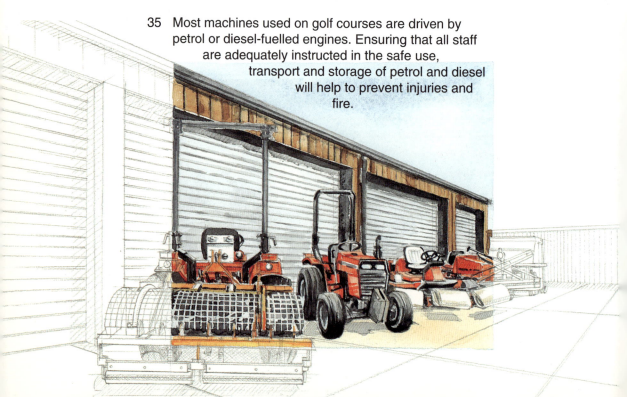

## TRACTORS

36 Tractors can overturn when working on slopes, uneven ground or near ditches. Incorrect loading, turning on slopes and unsafe driving will increase the risk of overturn. Remember there is no such thing as a 'safe' slope. Travel on grass slopes requires particular care. Providing tractors with a safety cab, frame or roll bar will give the driver protection if they overturn.

37 Drivers should be adequately trained, particularly to recognise potentially dangerous situations. The training should emphasise the need for care and concentration when working with tractors and, in particular, the importance of paying attention to changes in ground conditions, eg potholes, gravel or the turning circle load and speed which may affect the safety of the operation.

38  Routine checks and maintenance will help to ensure that:

  ❍ brakes on tractors and equipment are connected and working efficiently. Independent brakes should be linked whenever braked steering is not required;

  ❍ steering is maintained so that there is no excessive free movement and no unnecessary play on the front wheel bearings;

  ❍ tyres are inflated to the correct pressure and have adequate tread. They should not be used if they have suffered damage which could affect their safe use.

## POWER TAKE-OFF (PTO)

39 Every year people are killed or seriously injured in accidents involving PTO and PTO shafts. Many of these accidents would have been prevented if the PTO and PTO shaft had been correctly fitted with guards which were properly used and maintained. A tractor PTO and the PTO shaft of a machine can be extremely dangerous and require guarding unless safe by position and never approached when in motion or use. The guard and the PTO shaft should be properly maintained by regular lubrication in accordance with the manufacturer's instructions. If the guard is damaged in any way, the machine should be taken out of service until a new guard is fitted. Further information on the guarding of PTOs and PTO shafts is given in the free HSE leaflet *Power take-off and power take-off shafts*[5].

40 Many 'compact' tractors, ie the type used for grass maintenance, have a mid-mounted PTO drive facility as well as a rear PTO. The PTO drives are interlocked, ie a person must sit on the driving seat before you can drive the machine. Particular attention should be given to the maintenance of this safety device.

## Mowers

41  A wide range of mowers are used on golf courses and they vary from semi-mounted tractor trailed or gang mowers to specially designed self-propelled equipment. Mowers may be ground driven or powered through the tractor PTO. Where self-propelled mowers are used, because of their grip in certain situations, they should be driven very carefully during transport.

42  Mower blades are sharp and cause accidents. These usually occur when carrying out maintenance or clearing blockages and it is important that staff are trained and competent to carry out the task. Mower blades can detach themselves if not properly maintained or when not changed at intervals specified by manufacturers. Many self-propelled mowers are designed to ensure that the blades cease to rotate when the operator leaves the driving seat. This device should be well maintained to ensure that it works every time. It is important to check that the blades have stopped rotating before any adjustment is carried out on the machine. In all cases if any adjustment is required to or near the blades the machine should be

switched off and, if necessary, the power supply isolated. This also applies to smaller pedestrian-controlled mowers. Rotary mowers are particularly hazardous if allowed to rotate when the machine is stationary. When buying a new pedestrian-controlled rotary mower ensure that it is fitted with a brake to stop the rotation of the blades when the power is disconnected.

43  Rotary mowers present a particular hazard if the guards around the blade are removed or damaged. The hover type of mower which is often used to cut steep banks is also dangerous if not used according to the manufacturer's instructions. Steep banks should not be cut with rigid bladed rotary mowers. There have been a number of serious injuries to operators who have slipped when operating on a steep slope. If operators slip it is possible for their feet to slide under the mower and come in contact with the rotating blades. Wearing steel toe capped boots with good grip will help to prevent serious injuries.

## Turf scarifiers, slitters and spiking equipment

44  All guards should be properly maintained and in position at all times. No-one, apart from the operator should be in close proximity to the machine while it is in use. Before attempting any maintenance of the machine or guards, the power should be disconnected and all moving parts stopped. The operator should be aware of and follow the manufacturer's instructions for safe operation.

## Groomers

45  These machines are designed to carry out a number of functions, eg mowing, scarifying and brushing, in one operation and may also collect the debris and cuttings at the same time. They have sophisticated hydraulic controls and it is important that these are carefully maintained, particularly those used to lift part of the equipment.

## BRUSH CUTTERS, BRUSH SAWS AND GRASS TRIMMERS

46   Brush cutters are used to clear out dense undergrowth or scrubland and can be used to fell small trees and bushes. Brush saws are fitted with a small circular saw blade designed to cut wood and are driven by a petrol engine. The blades are guarded to prevent material being thrown out by the cutting action, injuring the operator. Operators should ensure that there are no other people within 10 metres of the working area. The operation of this machine requires considerable training, skill and experience. Operators should wear hearing protection and eye protection. Sturdy footwear offering a good grip and trousers offering protection against grass juices or wet vegetation are recommended.

47  These machines should be properly maintained by a competent person. The blade should be sharpened in accordance with the manufacturer's instructions and should be regularly examined and immediately discarded if there is any evidence of cracking or overheating.

48  Some brush cutters can be converted to a grass trimmer, ie a machine that has a fast revolving nylon line used to cut long grass close to walls, fences, plants etc. Although less dangerous than a brush cutter, they still can cause accidents, including injuries to the eye and it is therefore advisable to wear eye and hearing protection. Before converting a trimmer to a brush saw by fitting a circular saw type blade, it is important that the manufacturer confirms that the machine is capable of being used in this mode and that adequate guards are available to ensure that it complies with current safety standards.

49  Different guards are normally provided for brush cutter blade, brush saw blade and trimmer. It is important to fit correct guards which match the cutting attachment. A trimmer needs to be fitted with a barrier if it is used with a saw or brush cutter blade.

## FERTILISER SPREADERS

50  Mounted spreaders can affect the stability of the tractor when used on sloping or uneven ground. All tractor drivers required to use this type of equipment should be trained in its use and be aware of the effect of the spreader on the stability of the tractor. Drivers should be made aware of the risks of becoming trapped between the tractor and mounted equipment such as spreaders.

## SAND GRADERS

51  Most golf courses have machinery to extract stones and pebbles from sand used to fill bunkers or to mix soils or other materials to make a compost mulch.

52  If the machine is power driven, all guards should be kept in place to ensure that no-one can come in contact with any of the moving parts. Check with your supplier to ensure that your machine complies with current safety standards.

## OTHER MACHINERY

53  Golf clubs may use or hire other machines such as drainage machines, post hole borers, chain-saws etc. If these machines are used very infrequently it will probably be safer to engage a contractor to carry out the work. Competence in any task is achieved by training and experience. It is very difficult to achieve an acceptable level of competence when an operator, even though fully trained, only uses the equipment infrequently. Chain-saws in particular are dangerous even when properly maintained and equipped with all safety devices.

54  It is important that the chain-saw is checked thoroughly before use to ensure that all guards are in position and in good repair, the chain, guide bar and sprockets are undamaged and all external fittings are secure. Cutting chains with only kickback guard, eg guard links, are recommended. The chain should be correctly tensioned and sharpened according to the manufacturer's specifications. The lubrication system should be working and the chain brake tested to ensure that it works properly. The HSE leaflet *Safety with chainsaws* [6] contains useful information on chain-saw use and personal protective equipment.

55  Anyone using a chain-saw even for a short period, should wear the full protective clothing. This includes: safety helmet, face visor, hearing protection, clothing that is close fitting, chain-saw operator's gloves, leg protection and chain-saw operator's safety boots. All users should be properly trained. Information on training courses is available from the Forestry Aboricultural Safety Council; the Agricultural Training Board - Landbase or the National Proficiency Tests Council (see Appendix 5).

## SPRINKLER SYSTEMS

56  Most courses now have some form of sprinkler system, usually operated by an electric pump through a control panel. There can be a problem from connecting up to a sprinkler system if there is hydraulic pressure, as pipes can fly off and hit the operator. The electrical part of the installation should comply with the Electricity at Work Regulations 1989. The installation should be carried out by a competent person and staff using the equipment should be trained in its safe use.

## Personal transport

57  Because of the distances involved, many greenkeepers have transport available to move them round the course. This can be by tractor, tractor and trailer, all terrain vehicle or golf buggy. Apart from the golf buggy, most machines are designed only to seat the operator and it is important that other people should not ride on machines or tractors except on a trailer. In particular children should not be allowed to ride on machines. Golf buggies normally have seats for two people and light equipment can be carried in comparative safety. If the club provide all terrain vehicles (ATVs) for personal transport at work the operator should be trained in their safe use, wear suitable clothing (ie not loose fitting) and suitable head protection which preferably provides protection for the neck as well. Motor cycle helmets to BS 6658:1985 are adequate for this purpose. Care should be taken to secure any tools or equipment carried on the ATV.

58 ATVs used for spraying pesticides can expose the operator to high levels of pesticides, eg spraying with a following or head wind, with high booms, or in a figure eight or similar pattern. Ways to reduce the risk include considering alternative methods of control or application and selecting the pesticide that gives the least risk to operators and the environment.

# HEALTH AND SAFETY *in* GOLF COURSE MANAGEMENT AND MAINTENANCE

HS(G) 79
ISBN 0 7176 0689 9

### Erratum

On p 35 the second sentence should read 'COSHH will cover those substances which are very toxic, toxic (see Figure 1), corrosive (see Figure 2) or harmful, irritant (see Figure 3).'

## OCCUPATIONAL HEALTH

### SUBSTANCES

...rdous substances which are used on the ...ill be subject to the Control of ...Hazardous to Health Regulations 1988 ...ee Appendix 1). COSHH will cover those ...which are very toxic, toxic (see Figure 1),

Figure 2

Figure 3

...ant (see Figure 2) or corrosive (see ...ome pesticides may be hazardous ...under COSHH, as may be cleaning ...oils or other substances used in ...Not all hazardous substances come in ...kages. Some, such as wood dust, may be ...process being carried out. Others may ...the particular environment, for instance ...may present a hazard if rats and open ...es are present. Complying with COSHH ...essing the risks, deciding what ...are needed, and preventing or controlling ...y necessary controls should be used and ...informed of the precautions to be taken.

...rmation about products may be found on ...the information is not readily available ...el or supplier's advisory leaflet, then a ...for that product may be obtained from the ...manufacturer. They have a legal duty to ...information.

OCCUPATIONAL HEALTH

61 The assessment of risks does not have to be written down.  However, many employers find it useful to do so, especially when dealing with more hazardous substances, where the control measures are complex, or where it is necessary for communication purposes. The key element is that the assessment is suitable and sufficient, this means that the detail and expertise with which it is carried out are in proportion to the nature and degree of risk arising from the work.

62 As with all management tasks, the process should be kept under review to ensure that appropriate control measures are being carried out and to check whether there have been any significant changes to working procedures, new materials etc which would merit reassessment.

## USE OF PESTICIDES

63  Pesticide products are wide ranging and include fungicides, herbicides, insecticides, public hygiene pest control products, rodenticides and wood preservatives. Their sale, supply, advertisement, storage and use is prohibited under the Control of Pesticides Regulations 1986 (COPR) unless they have been approved (see Appendix 1).

64  Only approved pesticides should be used and the label should include a MAFF or HSE number. If you are unsure check with your supplier. The conditions of use are stated in every individual pesticide approval and are printed on the product label. The conditions of use should be followed. Anyone working with pesticides is required to be competent (see section on *Training and competence* - paragraphs 9-13).

65  Some pesticides are approved for 'agricultural use' (if you are unsure - check with your supplier). If these products are used the operator may require a certificate of competence. *The Code of Practice for the use of approved pesticides in amenity and industrial areas*[7] provides further information on user training and certification and classification of pesticides.

66  If pesticide product labels have become unreadable, eg faded, the pesticide should be disposed of safely. Local waste regulation authorities can give advice on acceptable disposal routes, including details of local companies offering such services. The waste regulation authorities are:

   ○ in England, county councils (for non-metropolitan areas) and district councils or single purpose waste authorities (for metropolitan areas);

   ○ in Wales, district councils;

   ○ in Scotland, district or island councils.

67  All pesticides should be stored in a suitably constructed, secure bin, cabinet, chest or vault capable of resisting fire for at least 30 minutes and robust enough to withstand reasonably foreseeable accidental impact and be secure against theft and vandalism. The store needs to be fitted with a sump which will retain the total capacity plus 10% of the contents stored, in the event of all containers failing simultaneously (eg in the case of a fire). It should not be sited in a staff room or office and if kept outside it needs to be waterproof. The pesticide store should be identified by a cautionary warning sign and smoking prohibited in the area. For large quantities of pesticides, containers specifically manufactured to comply with the legislative requirements for storage are available on the market. Otherwise a purpose-built pesticide store should be constructed or a suitable building converted. See *Storage of approved pesticides: Guidance for farmers and other professional users* [8].

## NOISE AND VIBRATION

68  Noise at excessive levels can be a major health hazard. It can accelerate the normal hearing loss which occurs as we grow older.

69  Vibration transmitted directly to the hands can cause a condition known as 'vibration white finger' in which blood supply to the hands and fingers is affected, especially in cold conditions. Whole body vibration (eg received by someone sitting on a machine) can cause back problems.

70   Less obviously both noise and vibration can contribute to stress at work.

71   Risks and Action Levels will depend on how long people are exposed to noise as well as how loud it is. If people find that they need to shout to be heard by someone two metres away, or if their ears are ringing after a period of noisy work, there might be a noise problem.

72   Noise and vibration can be controlled by buying machines and tools with low noise and vibration characteristics and maintaining them so that noise and vibration does not increase. Other measures include reducing the duration of exposure by shortening the period an operator works with the machine. This can be organised by job rotation or by planning your system of work to ensure that noisy machines are used only for short periods at a time.

73   Information on the noise regulations is set out in Appendix 1.

# APPENDIX 1
# KNOW THE LAW

## THE HEALTH AND SAFETY AT WORK ETC ACT 1974

1. All employers have a general duty under the Health and Safety at Work Act Etc 1974 (HSW Act) to ensure, so far as is reasonably practicable, that the health, safety and welfare at work of their employees is protected. This duty includes:

   ○ providing and maintaining machinery, equipment, appliances and systems of work that are safe and without risks to health;

   ○ ensuring that articles and substances are used, handled, stored and transported safely and without risks to health;

   ○ providing the necessary information, instruction, training and supervision to ensure the health and safety at work of all employees;

   ○ maintaining a workplace that is safe and without risks to health; and

   ○ providing and maintaining a working environment which is safe, without risks to health, and which has adequate facilities and arrangements for employees' welfare at work.

2. Under the HSW Act, employees also have a legal duty to take reasonable care of themselves and others and to co-operate with their employers regarding their legal obligations. In addition, the Act will apply to all contractors hired to work on the golf course. They are required to ensure that their activities are not a danger to themselves or others.

3   Employers will also have a responsibility for the health and safety of visitors, eg members of the public, self-employed people or contractor's employees working with them who may be affected by work activities under the contractor's control. This may entail co-operating and exchanging information with all those employers working on the golf course premises.

4   Employers with five or more employees are required to prepare a written statement of their general policy, organisation and arrangements for the health and safety at work of their employees. The statement and any revision of it should be brought to the attention of all the employees.

5   The Health and Safety Executive will undertake the enforcement of health and safety legislation if the golf course is owned and controlled by a local authority. The local District or Metropolitan Council will be responsible for the enforcement of health and safety legislation if the golf course is privately owned. Both enforcing authorities will be able to provide information and advice on particular areas of concern.

## MANAGEMENT OF HEALTH AND SAFETY AT WORK REGULATIONS 1992

6   The Management of Health and Safety at Work Regulations 1992 are aimed mainly at improving health and safety management. Their main provisions are designed to encourage a more systematic approach to dealing with health and safety. The Regulations require employers amongst other duties, to:

   ○ assess the risks to the health and safety of their employees and others who may be affected by their work activity;

○ make arrangements for putting into practice the health and safety measures that the risk assessment shows to be necessary. These arrangements should cover planning, organisation, control, monitoring and review.

7   Specific risk assessments already carried out under other health and safety legislation, eg COSSH and The Manual Handling Operations Regulations do not need to be repeated or supplemented; they will form part of the overall risk assessment.

8   The Regulations further expand the general duties under HSW Act by requiring employers to take into account their employees' capabilities, as regards health and safety, when giving them tasks to do, eg previous training, knowledge and experience.

9   Further information is given in the Approved Code of Practice *Management of health and safety at work* [9].

## HEALTH AND SAFETY (FIRST AID) REGULATIONS 1981

10  Under the Health and Safety (First Aid) Regulations 1981 all workplaces should have first-aid material in a clearly identified box and an appointed person(s) to ensure the proper management of injuries or illnesses at work. The first-aid provision will depend on a variety of factors including: the nature and degree of the hazards at work; whether there is shift work; what medical services are available; and the number of employees. The HSE booklet *First aid at work* [10] explains the requirements and provides guidance to help employers meet their obligations.

## THE REPORTING OF INJURIES, DISEASES AND DANGEROUS OCCURRENCES REGULATIONS 1985

11  The Reporting of Injuries, Diseases and Dangerous Occurrences Regulations 1985 (RIDDOR) require employers, people in control of premises and in some cases the self-employed to report certain types of injury, occupational ill health and dangerous occurrences to their enforcing authority. Who is the enforcing authority is explained in paragraph 4 of this Appendix.

12  There are two ways in which injuries and incidents have to be reported to an enforcing authority and these depend on the severity and the potential for harm:

(a)  (i) if an *employee or a visitor* dies or suffers a specified injury in an accident arising from or in connection with work; or

(ii) there is a dangerous occurrence.

Then the employer should notify the enforcing authority forthwith by the quickest practicable means, normally by telephone, and within seven days send a written report using Form 2508 (available from HSE Books). Reports are required whether or not the person concerned is an employee.

(b) where *any one at work* is off work or cannot carry out their normal duties for more than three consecutive days as a result of an accident at work, this is also reportable and the employer has seven days in which to send a report to the enforcing authority.

13  Further information is given in the HSE booklet *A guide to the Reporting of Injuries, Diseases, and Dangerous Occurrences Regulations 1985* [11].

## THE WORKPLACE (HEALTH, SAFETY AND WELFARE) REGULATIONS 1992

14  The Workplace (Health, Safety and Welfare) Regulations 1992 aim to ensure that workplaces meet the health, safety and welfare needs of each member of the workforce. Premises built after the 1 January 1993, or modifications, extensions, or conversions to existing premises after that date, will have to comply with the Regulations. All other premises will be required to comply from 1 January 1996. These Regulations give more detail to the general duties of employers under the Health and Safety at Work Etc Act 1974.

15  Further information is given in the Approved Code of Practice *Workplace health, safety and welfare* [12].

## PERSONAL PROTECTIVE EQUIPMENT AT WORK (PPE) REGULATIONS 1992

16  The Personal Protective Equipment at Work Regulations 1992 require employers to make sure that suitable personal protective equipment is provided and used by employees wherever there is a risk to health and safety that cannot be adequately controlled by other means. This includes, eg the provision of safety footwear where there is a risk of foot injuries, headgear where there is a risk of head injuries or suitable outdoor clothing if the job involves working outside in adverse weather conditions that could prejudice the health and safety of the employee.

17  Further guidance on the Regulations is given in the HSE booklet *Personal protective equipment at work* [13].

## THE MANUAL HANDLING OPERATIONS REGULATIONS 1992

18   The Manual Handling Operations Regulations 1992 require employers to take reasonably practicable steps to avoid manual handling activities where there is a risk of injury. Where such manual handling cannot be avoided, the employer should make an assessment and take appropriate measures to reduce the risk of injury to the lowest level reasonably practicable. The assessment will form part of the overall risk assessment required by the Management of Health and Safety at Work Regulations 1992.

19   Further guidance on the Regulations is given in the HSE booklet *Manual Handling* [14].

## THE PROVISION AND USE OF WORK EQUIPMENT REGULATIONS 1992

20   The Provision and Use of Work Equipment Regulations 1992 were implemented to pull together existing regulations which governed the use of equipment at work. Instead of fragmentary regulations covering individual pieces of equipment, these Regulations place general duties on employers and list minimum requirements for work equipment to deal with selective hazards, whatever the industry. The date of application will depend on whether the equipment is new, existing, second-hand, hired or leased. All work equipment in use at the golf course will be subject to these Regulations.

21   Further guidance on the Regulations is given in the HSE booklet *Work Equipment* [15].

KNOW THE LAW

## CONTROL OF SUBSTANCES HAZARDOUS TO HEALTH REGULATIONS 1988

22  The Control of Substances Hazardous to Health Regulations 1988 (COSHH) require employers to ensure that exposure of their employees to hazardous substances is either prevented, or if this is not reasonably practicable, adequately controlled. Under these Regulations some of the employer's responsibilities extend to people, other than employees, who may be affected by the work activity.

23  The employer is required to carry out an assessment of the health risks which might arise from the various work activities, and to state the action they intend to take to prevent or control the exposure of their workforce to hazardous substances, and to comply with other requirements of the Regulations.

24  The Regulations require all employers to:

○ assess the risk to their employees and others from exposure to hazardous substances at work and so establish whether precautions are needed. This will include determining what substances are present and in what form; how are they handled; what harmful effects are possible; who is likely to be affected;

○ introduce appropriate measures to prevent or control the exposure to those substances where a risk has been identified which needs to be controlled, such as substitution by a safer product;

○ ensure that control measures are used and that equipment is properly maintained and procedures observed;

○ where necessary, monitor the exposure of the workers and carry out an appropriate form of surveillance of their health;

○ inform, instruct and train employees about the risks and the precautions to be taken.

25 Practical guidance on COSHH is given in some detail in its associated Approved Codes of Practice[16] and in the Approved Code of Practice *The safe use of pesticides for non-agricultural purposes*[17].

## THE NOISE AT WORK REGULATIONS 1988

26 These Regulations are intended to reduce hearing damage caused by loud noise. They require employers to take action when noise exposure reaches an 85 dB(A) 'First Action Level' and further action if it reaches 90 dB(A) 'Second' or 140 dB(A) 'Peak' Action Levels. At the First Action Level, employers have to provide ear protectors to any employees who want them. Control of levels above 90 dB(A) has to be by means other than ear protectors where reasonably practicable.

27 Further information is given in the HSE publication *Introducing the Noise at Work Regulations: a brief guide to the requirements for controlling noise at workplaces*[18].

## THE CONTROL OF PESTICIDE REGULATIONS 1986

28 The Control of Pesticide Regulations 1986 covers the sale, supply and advertisement of pesticides as well as the storage and use of pesticides such as fungicides, herbicides, insecticides, public hygiene pest control products, rodenticides and wood preservatives. They were made under the Food and Environment Protection Act 1985, and are intended to protect the health of human beings, animals and plants, and to protect the environment. Everyone who uses pesticides should be competent in the tasks undertaken and should have received adequate information and training to use pesticides safely and legally.

47

KNOW THE LAW

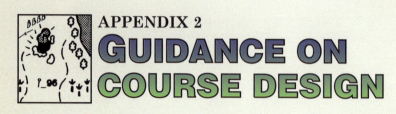

# APPENDIX 2
# GUIDANCE ON COURSE DESIGN

Note: While this advice is not mandatory under health and safety law, it will be useful when considering design issues and the effect they may have on others.

1   When designing a course, special consideration may need to be given to footpaths and bridleways (public rights of way). These may not be immediately obvious and golf clubs and course designers should consult the Highway Authority about the existence of public rights of way on the site as this may influence the design. Discussions with health and safety officers from the local District Council, parish or community councils, and local path users' groups, eg the Ramblers' Association etc will help to ensure that the layout of the course takes into account the rights of way network and its safety implications for users.

2   The following check-list will be helpful when designing a new course:

 Is the course situated alongside a public highway or residential property? If so the greens and tees may need to be structured to reduce the possibility of a wayward shot landing on the highway. This could be achieved in a number of ways:

○ position the greens away from the highway or residential property;

○ position tees so that all tee shots are played away from the highway or residential property;

○ ensure that the heaviest rough and worst bunkers are in the direction of the highway or residential property with the easier route in the other direction to encourage golfers to play away from the hazard;

○ use mature trees and undergrowth behind green to catch the wayward ball;

○ position bunkers between green and highway or residential property to ensure that bunker shots, especially close to the green, are played away from the highway or residential property. For the same reason bunkers should not be positioned where a 'flyer' will clear the green and reach the highway or residential property;

○ if it is impossible to incorporate all these points in the design of the course it may be necessary to build appropriate fencing and screening to reduce the risk to the public using the highway or residential property.

GUIDANCE ON COURSE DESIGN

🚩 2    Are there steep slopes which could create a hazard to the greenkeeper carrying out regular maintenance of the course? If the slope is close to the fairway you may wish to consider either levelling it off slightly or sowing rough grass and planting shrubs to remove the need for grass-cutting or other maintenance.

🚩 3    Will the trees and shrubs require regular pruning? Keeping maintenance of trees and shrubs to a minimum will reduce the need to use chain-saws and brush cutters. Trees can create serious safety problems when being felled or pruned.

🚩 4    Is there good access to all parts of the course for maintenance machinery including tractors and trailers? Are all bridges over streams designed to allow such machinery to cross in safety?

🚩 5    Is the course designed to allow the use of ride-on golf buggies in the future? Some courses have specific roadways for this type of vehicle. In the absence of clearly defined roadways it may be very difficult to mark recommended routes on traditional courses.

🚩 6    Are greens situated to ensure that players putting out are not at risk from wayward shots from adjoining tees?

🚩 7    Has the general public right of access to the course? This should be considered in the general course design to reduce, as far as reasonably practicable, the risk to the public. It may be necessary to display clear instructions to the public and to golfers on the safe use of the course.

## Practice areas

3   When choosing or designing practice areas you may need to take care to ensure that players using them are not at risk from golf balls from adjoining parts of the course. Displaying a clear set of rules and instructions, relating to the safe use of this facility, will help to prevent accidents. This is particularly important when the area is used by the golf club professional to teach groups of players. For example, temporary suspension of play on the practice area will enable employees to collect golf balls without risk of being hit.

## GOLF DRIVING RANGES

4   The playing facilities usually consist of a single storey building with a series of open fronted bays facing a large area with target greens set at different distances from the bays. Safe working practices would include:

○ ensuring that there is no risk to people entering or leaving individual bays while other bays are in use or at risk when using the individual bays, ie there is adequate screening in order to prevent users being struck by balls which have not been correctly hit;

○ displaying clear written rules on the use of the facility and providing an adequate level of supervision at all times;

○ preventing entry to the target area in front of the bays;

○ making special arrangements to allow safe collection of the balls, including preventing manual collection until all practice has stopped. When collecting using a suitably protected vehicle which collects the balls mechanically, there should be emergency arrangements to suspend all play if the machine breaks down and the operator is required to leave the cab;

○ undertaking maintenance of the target area when play is suspended.

## APPENDIX 3
# REFERENCES

1 *Train to survive* 1992

2 *BS 7671:1991 Regulations for electrical installations* Institution of Electrical Engineers 16th Edition 1991 ISBN 0 852965 57 5

3 *Avoidance of danger from overhead electrical lines* GS 6 (rev) 1991 ISBN 0 11 885568 5

4 BS 5304:1988 *Safety of machinery* 1988 ISBN 0 580 16344 X

5 *Power take-off and power take-off shafts* AS 24 1981 Free leaflet

6 *Safety with chainsaws* AS 20 1986 Free leaflet

7 *Code of Practice for the use of approved pesticides in amenity and industrial areas* 1991 National Association of Agricultural Contractors National Turfgrass Council ISBN 1 871140 12 9

8 *Storage of approved pesticides: Guidance for farmers and other professional users* CS 19 1988 ISBN 0 11 885406 2

9 *Management of health and safety at work: Management of Health and Safety at Work Regulations 1992. Approved Code of Practice* L21 1992 ISBN 0 7176 0412 8

10 *First aid at work: Health and Safety (First Aid) Regulations 1981* COP 42 1990 ISBN 0 7176 0426 8

11 *A guide to the Reporting of Injuries, Diseases and Dangerous Occurrences Regulations 1985* HS(R)23 1986 ISBN 0 7176 0432 2

12  *Workplace health, safety and welfare. Workplace (Health, Safety and Welfare) Regulations 1992. Approved Code of Practice and Guidance*
L24 1992 ISBN 0 7176 0413 6

13  *Personal protective equipment at work. Personal Protective Equipment at Work Regulations 1992. Guidance on Regulations*
L25 1992 ISBN 0 7176 0415 2

14  *Manual handling. Manual Handling Operations Regulations 1992. Guidance on Regulations*
L23 1992 ISBN 0 7176 0411 X

15  *Work equipment. Provision and Use of Work Equipment Regulations 1992. Guidance on the Regulations* L22 1992 ISBN 0 7176 0414 4

16  *Control of Substances Hazardous to Health and Control of Carcinogenic Substances. Control of Substances Hazardous to Health Regulations 1988. Approved Codes of Practice*
L5 4th ed 1993 ISBN 0 7176 0427 6

17  *The safe use of pesticides for non-agricultural purpose. Approved Code of Practice*
L9 1991 ISBN 0 11 885673 1

18  *Introducing the Noise at Work Regulations: a brief guide to the requirements for controlling noise at workplaces*
IND(G)75L (rev) 1989 Free leaflet

## APPENDIX 4
# FURTHER READING

*COSHH: A brief guide for employers. The requirements of the Control of Substances Hazardous to Health (COSSH) Regulations 1988* IND(G)136(L) 1993 Free leaflet

*Essentials of health and safety at work* (rev) 1994
ISBN 0 7176 0716 X

*Flexible leads, plugs, sockets etc* GS 37 1985
ISBN 0 11 883519 X

*Getting to grips with manual handling. A short guide for employers* IND(G)143(L) 1993 Free leaflet

*A Guide to the Health and Safety at Work etc Act 1974*
L1(rev) 1990 ISBN 0 7176 0441 1

*A guide to producing a farm COSHH assessment* IAC/L81 1993

*Health and Safety at Work etc Act 1974: advice to employees* HSC5 1991 Free leaflet

*Health and Safety at Work etc Act 1974: advice to employers* HSC3 1990 Free leaflet

*It's your job to manage safety* IND(G)103(L) 1991 Free leaflet

*Lighten the load: guidance for employees on musculoskeletal disorders* IND(G)110(L) 1991
Free leaflet

*Lighten the load: guidance for employers on musculoskeletal disorders* IND(G)109(L) 1991 Free leaflet

*Maintaining portable and transportable electrical equipment* HS(G)107 1994 ISBN 0 7176 0715 1

FURTHER READING

*Memorandum of guidance on the Electricity at Work Regulations 1989* HS(R)25 1989 ISBN 0 11 883963 2

*New Health and Safety at Work Regulations* IND(G)124(L) 1992 Free leaflet

*Prevention of tractors overturning* AS 22(rev) 1988 Free leaflet

*Reporting under RIDDOR* HSE 24 1992 Free leaflet

*The safe use of portable electrical apparatus (electrical safety)* PM 32(rev) 1990 ISBN 0 11 885590 5

*A step by step guide to COSHH assessment* HS(G)97 1993 ISBN 0 11 886379 7

*Successful health and safety management* HS(G) 65 1991
ISBN 0 7176 0425 X

*Tractor-trailer safety brakes* AS 16(rev) 1988 Free leaflet

*Watch your step: prevention of slipping, tripping and falling accidents at work* 1985 ISBN 0 11 883782 6

*Writing a policy statement: advice to employers* HSC6 (rev) 1985 Free leaflet

*Writing your health and safety policy statement* (rev) 1989 ISBN 0 7176 0424 1

HSE free and priced publications are available from HSE Books (see inside back cover for details). Further information on HSE publications can be obtained from:

HSE Information Centre
Broad Lane
Sheffield
S3 7HQ

Tel: 0742 892345
Fax: 0742 892333

British Standards are available from:

British Standards Institution
Linford Wood
Milton Keynes
MK14 6LE

Tel: 0908 220022
Fax: 0908 320856

# APPENDIX 5
# OTHER SOURCES OF INFORMATION

Agricultural Engineers Association, Samuelson House, Paxton Road, Orton Centre, Peterborough PE2 5LT

The Agricultural Training Board, Stoneleigh Park Pavilion, National Agricultural Centre, Kenilworth, Warwickshire, CV8 7UG

Arboricultural Safety Council, Ampfield House, Ampfield, Romsey, Hants SO51 9PA

The Association of Golf Secretaries, 7A Beaconsfield Road, Weston-Super-Mare, Avon BS23 1YE

The British and International Golf Greenkeepers Association, Aldwark Manor, Aldwark, Alne, York, YO6 2NF

British Safety Council National Safety Centre, Chancellor's Road, London, W6 9RS

English Golf Union, 1 - 3 Upper King Street, Leicester LE1 6XF

Forestry Safety Council, Forestry Commission, 231 Corstosphine Road, Edinburgh EH12 7AT

The Greenkeepers Training Committee, Aldwark Manor, Aldwark, Alne, York YO6 2NF

HSE Pesticides Registration Section, Magdalen House, Stanley Precinct, Bootle L20 3QZ

MAFF Pesticides Safety Directorate, Rothamsted, Harpenden, Herts AL5 2SS

The National Proficiency Test Council, 10th Street,
National Agricultural Centre, Stoneleigh, Warwickshire,
CV8 2LG

Rights of Way Officer, The Ramblers Association,
1 - 5 Wandsworth Road, London SW8 2XX

The Royal and Ancient Golf Club of St Andrews,
St Andrews, Fife  KY16 9JD

Royal Society for the Prevention of Accidents,
Canon House, the Priory, Queensway, Birmingham,
B4 6BS

Scottish Golf Union, The Cottage, 181a Whitehouse Road,
Barnton, Edinburgh EH14 6BY

Welsh Golf Union, Powys House, Cwmbran, Gwent
NT44 1PD

OTHER SOURCES OF INFORMATION

  Printed and published by
the Health and Safety Executive C80 6/94